CW00660960

Marian Cole

With best wishes

Peter.

Christmas 1997.

ROBIN LOWES

TALES OF FOUR SEASONS

A light-hearted ramble through the seasons

ROBIN LOWES

TALES OF FOUR SEASONS

A light-hearted ramble through the seasons

With best wishes
Robin Lowes.

PARDOE BLACKER

British Library Cataloguing in Publication Data:
A catalogue record for this book is available
from the British Library

ISBN 1-897739-01-X

Published in the UK in 1997 by
Pardoe Blacker Publishing Limited
Shawlands Court
Newchapel Road
Lingfield
Surrey RH7 6BL

1 3 5 7 9 8 6 4 2

Set in Photina
Designed and produced by Pardoe Blacker Publishing Limited
Lingfield · Surrey

Colour origination by Collective Colour Limited
Printed in Britain by
Balding+Mansell

Contents

Acknowledgements

I MUST FIRST OF ALL THANK His Grace, the Duke of Northumberland for his most generous foreword.

Sport and nature go side by side and the many who appreciate this increase their overall enjoyment many times over.

I must also thank Elwyn Blacker of Pardoe Blacker, the publishers, for his suggestions, help and enthusiasm, which has been positively infectious – and these comments apply to the whole staff of Pardoe Blacker. This book would have got nowhere without them. I must also pay tribute to my wife's 'Winter' verse – composed over a midnight glass of whisky – though she prefers to remain anonymous! Her encouragement too has been tremendous.

My thanks to Ian MacAlpine-Leny for allowing the reproduction of the photograph he took of me whilst we fished together for steelhead in north British Columbia.

Foreword

I HAVE KNOWN Robin Lowes and his family for many years, enjoyed days chasing his grouse, ptarmigan and sea-trout and admired his approach to conservation and estate management.

Robin has spent a lifetime with gun, rod and camera close by his side, whether on his beloved patches in Scotland and Sussex, or travelling to far-flung parts of the world where he has recorded on film and mind, his fascinating experiences and observations of nature.

The combination of a passion for wildlife, and great talent for photography, makes this book delightful in every way. Personal reflections and anecdotes combine with a powerful knowledge to make an amusing and interesting read, whilst the photographs are just breath-taking.

This is one of those books that will always enthral the reader and will certainly find an honoured place in my library.

Northumberland

THE DUKE OF NORTHUMBERLAND

Introduction

THIS IS A LIGHT HEARTED RAMBLE through the seasons of the year. Everyone has their favourite season, but each has its own appeal and beauty.

I have started in the winter when the country was covered in snow – an event that, as the years progress, seems with global warming, an increasingly rare event. Forget the dull dreary winter days of rain when even your labradors prefer to stand at the front door, and say no thank you to their daily walk. Dank dark days soon give way to crisp clear ones, and a weak winter sun can transform the countryside as if by magic.

Spotted flycatcher on the look out for insects.

Amidst the high hills.

Blackthorn in spring.

The days soon lengthen, and with them comes the song of blackbirds – first above all others – that gradually swells into the dawn chorus that heralds the spring.

A warm sunny February day will persuade the first Brimstone butterflies to take wing and bumble-bees to work from dawn to dusk.

In no time at all daffodils are swaying gently in the breeze, the first swallows arrive, and the drumming of a woodpecker and the cuckoo's familiar call reverberate and echo across the land. By the end of April the woods are carpeted with bluebells whose fragrance is almost overpowering, whilst trees and hedgerows burst into every shade of green in extraordinary beauty and freshness.

How fortunate we are to live in a country of such marked seasons, when spring lasts months, not a short day or two as in the Arctic. Summer then turns back to winter with scarcely a moment for the glories of our autumn with its crisp sunny days, morning and evening mist, a wild harvest of blackberries and mushrooms, trees laden with fruit and berries, but above all colours – from red to gold. It vies with spring as my favourite time of year.

The stories cover a series of episodes that have occurred over the years. I hope lovers of nature will enjoy them as much as my family and I have done.

WINTER

The bustle of summer and autumn is done.
There is time to rest and for time to come.
There is beauty there beyond fair share
as diamonds shine in the midnight air,
Spider webs silvered in the cold
to show the season has grown old.
As plants we are for rest and renew,
Come – think and dream and plan anew.

ANON

Footprints in the snow

SNOW LAY ALL AROUND US covering lawn, flower beds and woods with a glittering white mantle, still inches deep eight weeks after the first heavy falls. A further sprinkling during the night revealed the fresh tracks of a fox which had circumnavigated the house by way of the flagstone path before vaulting our five-barred gate into the lane above.

The identity of our prowler would have been elementary even to Dr Watson, for a fox's tracks are unmistakable – his pad marks are placed one in front of the other so that the general effect is, unlike a dog's, almost a straight line of footprints.

LEFT: *A winter meet – where foxes met.*

OPPOSITE: *Squirrel tracks crossing a log.*

Rabbits everywhere!

Rabbit tracks were everywhere as if a whole army of them had been at work crossing and re-crossing each other. But probably there were only one or two about as a single rabbit will leave numerous prints behind him in a night. In their search for food, little had escaped their attention – young apple trees had been stripped of bark, and where the rabbits could not reach, a hare had taken over, his tracks showing his point of entry and exit into the orchard as plainly as if he had been in full view the whole time.

Hay fed to cattle in the field above the marsh had attracted flocks of finches and other birds: pheasant tracks led to it from all angles in their search for food. All must have been near starvation from the prolonged cold and, alas, many had passed the point of no return.

Farther down, a broad ditch separates field from marsh. Completely frozen over, a heron's tracks appeared from nowhere in the virgin snow on the bank above, marking his landing place, then showed where he had jumped down and stalked along the ice edge before taking off again after his apparently fruitless search.

But perhaps the most intriguing tracks were produced by a pair of otters walking side by side on an ice-covered river in the Scottish Highlands. A light powdering of snow had covered the ice, but the wind had blown much of it away, obliterating their usual tail marks in the process. The imprints of

Two otters walked side by side over this frozen river.

Pheasant's tracks.

their pads, however, had frozen in remarkable clarity. Down river their tracks had separated, then come together again as they journeyed on. But for their tracks on the snow-covered ice, we would not have known they were there.

Farther up river, the fast-flowing stream had not completely frozen over. In places chunks of ice had broken off and lay at grotesque angles as the water level had dropped, framing gaps through which an otter could find easy access to and from the smaller pools.

Great travellers at any time, they, at least, in common with other predators, would find no difficulty in keeping alive, and two of them would have little trouble in catching the odd trout in such low water, and, for my part, they are always welcome. Indeed, we love our otters and would never begrudge them an occasional trout supper when their staple diet consists of eels, the arch villains of the spawning grounds.

Many years earlier in one very cold January I remember my father returned to tea buoyed up by witnessing a family of otters tobogganing down the steep side of a snow-covered bank by the river's edge. Time and again they slid into the water and raced up the bank to repeat the performance for the sheer fun of it. How encouraging now ('97) to know that they are on the increase in so many places and particularly in the Scottish Highlands.

If, for some, the extreme severity of winter tends to blur the general beauty such weather brings – and birdlife certainly suffers cruel loss – it is encouraging to observe much that has survived.

Whilst much of this took place in the memorable prolonged freeze of 1963, now more than thirty years on, and despite dire prophecies from time to time of cold winters to come, these have not materialised. Indeed it has been very much the reverse. Rain we have had in plenty, and never more than this winter of 93/94. Cold snaps in November prompt some meteorologist or other to gloomy forebodings, but they cannot have heard the old country saying 'If in November ice bears a duck, there will only thereafter be slush and muck'! – and it is surprising how true this saying often proves to be. It is late January as I write, and a good fall of snow would be really welcome, for one or more rabbits are invading the garden each night, and I have spent what seems like hours trying to find where they have breached our defences through the wire netting. A good snowfall would give the game away in no time at all!

Crumbs from the table

THERE CAN BE FEW PEOPLE living in the country these days who do not feed our wild birds throughout the winter months. No matter how large or small their garden, a peanut feeder, bird table with assorted seeds or a chunk of fat hung from the branch of a tree, or even corn thrown on the lawn or patio, will soon entice most of our garden birds.

At the start of the feeding season, to coincide with the first frosts of November, I was intrigued to find a great spotted woodpecker helping itself to peanuts that had only been hung up a few hours earlier. A pair of these beautiful birds had been regular visitors last winter, but how this bird discovered peanuts were on the menu again so quickly was quite extraordinary.

Throughout the winter months greenfinches and chaffinches and most of the tit family are present. Blue and great tits are nearly always the first arrivals, followed by coal tits and marsh and willow tits, the last two being almost impossible to distinguish, the only real way being their different song. The only other member of the family that frequents the woods all around us

Male great spotted woodpecker.

RIGHT: *Redwings feeding on discarded apples.*

A large family of blue tits on a peanut feeder.

is the delightful little long-tailed tit, whose whole family seem to spend their life playing follow my leader from branch to branch and tree to tree in their search for insects. They have, as yet, never ventured to our bird table or on to the chunks of fat hanging up nearby. When I was about to lunch with a friend in Wiltshire he rang up to say 'bring your camera as I have long-tailed tits feeding on the fat on my table'. A week later one of our neighbours told me he had experienced the same thing. It was the first time either of them had ever seen it. Perhaps habits are changing – I could understand it more readily if the weather had been severe, but it wasn't, so we live in hope that they will soon join our party.

Undoubtedly one of our favourite visitors is the nuthatch. With their dagger-like bills and sleek, streamlined appearance they are extremely handsome birds. They are the only birds I know that delight in descending head first in search of food – or for that matter eating in this way. One pair not only paid constant attendance to our offerings throughout the winter and early spring, but eventually rewarded us by nesting in a cavity of a stone wall which I had rebuilt after the 1987 hurricane. A hollow with a small entrance hole, made intentionally when rebuilding it, remained vacant for two seasons before they took the plunge!

The amount of bird food, particularly peanuts, that were consumed in our garden last winter – a very warm one in the south of England, seemed to me to be quite prodigious – well over 100 lb in weight. Compared to figures from America this itself could be termed peanuts, for their average apparently is some 350 lb of wild bird seed alone.

If variety is the spice of life it is certainly necessary if one is to attract more than just a handful of peanut-loving birds. Hedge sparrows, robins and many finches love all sorts of wild seeds, whilst blackbirds and thrushes, joined in severe weather by redwings and fieldfares, thrive on unwanted apples and scraps of bread. Even wagtails come around to feed on wild bird seed, a considerable change in diet from their normally insectivorous one of flies and other insects.

Nuthatch at nesting hole.

No wonder the peanuts have gone down so quickly!

In a prolonged freeze-up fresh water is vital, unless you are fortunate enough to have a stream nearby that does not ice up completely.

Really cold snaps increase the amount of food needed and often bring in the rarer winter migrants. Two or three winters ago we had a large number of chaffinches and one day on looking more closely found several bramblings amongst them, very easily overlooked.

Now we have a remarkable cock pheasant that has discovered wheat scattered on the lawn below the house. He has a dark bluish purple breast and the rest of him is almost midnight blue – a melanistic mutant that has gone slightly wrong! Although I have seen his like before, it is a most unusual colour, and when the sun shines on him he looks truly magnificent. Of course we get unwanted visitors – starlings being one of them – but the worst culprits are grey squirrels, which at times can be perfect pests. A friend living in Worcestershire has nightly visits from foxes, which come right up to his window in search of scraps, though these animals give him much pleasure to watch on a moonlit night, rather like the yellow-necked field mice that visit our bird table, sometimes in broad daylight. Perhaps we can consider ourselves fortunate compared to our American cousins, one of whom, living in the State of Ohio, had a visit from a black bear which sucked down the contents of his hummingbird feeder!

POSTSCRIPT

Since writing this a whole family of long-tailed tits, eight in all, paid a visit late one afternoon in early January (1997). After the prolonged icy weather they looked very thin and frail. One month later, to our great delight, they are regular visitors to the chunks of fat we shall continue to provide – at least until spring.

A yellow necked field mouse surprised in the apple shed.

SPRING

For winter's rains and ruins are over,
And all the season of snows and sins;
The days dividing lover and lover,
The light that loses, the night that wins;
And time remembered is grief forgotten,
And frosts are slain and flowers begotten,
And in green underwood and cover
Blossom by blossom the spring begins.

SWINBURNE: Atalanta in Calydon, 1865

Common or garden nesting sites

TOWARDS THE END of April or early May the postman knocks on our front door to deliver the letters. Apart from the odd registered package, our mail, at other times, is deposited by the front gate in a makeshift letter box, slotted at one end to accept deliveries and with a door at the other end for their removal – a box we inherited when we moved house.

The postman's knock varies with the season, but signals the return of a pair of great tits which take over the letter box for the next few weeks until their brood is safely reared and the birds have flown. With a bit of luck we revert to normal by the end of June. In the meantime, and for the convenience of all, a 7 lb biscuit tin suffices. Now our postman knows the form and uses this substitute letter box unfailingly, but alas, in our first season, the parish magazine was one day inadvertently 'posted' on top of

OPPOSITE: *Robin's nest in an old potato ridger.*

RIGHT: *A pair of great tits commandeer our letter box.*

the great tit as she sat on her clutch of eggs. Its contents obviously did not please her for she tore it to shreds, and, having expended her energy and ire, the poor bird deserted. So we have added a sign above the biscuit tin for those who can read – and keep our fingers crossed that all will be well in future.

It is surprising that great tits have selected this site year after year to make their nest, for the rather large slotted entrance hole provided by the box, which itself faces south, must be extremely draughty and much larger in size than that usually chosen.

In another part of the garden a home-made nesting box has been consistently cold-shouldered, due, I am sure, to the excessive diameter of the entrance hole. It hangs, unwanted, in a relatively quiet spot, until, one summer, compassion was bestowed on it in a most unwelcome form by a queen wasp.

The less common tree wasps have invaded the sanctity of our beehives on more than one occasion, entering through the top ventilation holes and hanging their nest from the roof. The bees, isolated by the cavity between sections and outer frames of the hive, went their way oblivious and undisturbed. The wasps make a beautiful little nest of paper-like wood particles, seldom bigger than a small apple and very brittle. These, unless protected from the elements as ours were, soon disintegrate in the autumn winds and rain, and this fact probably contributed to their choice of site.

During one winter's snow, another hive received a call from a visitor of quite a different colour, who this time took up residence on the ground floor, completely overstaying his welcome. As an amateur beekeeper I should have prevented the episode. However, our visitor, a long-tailed field mouse, whom I discovered only after the snows and frost had passed, must have been the envy of all his friends, having spent the most comfortable of coldest winters in a nest of leaves and grass in the bottom of the hive. This hive had fortunately been given plenty of room at the top, and all went well. In fact, the bees recovered from their fright and went on to harvest 30 lb of honey. The mouse it was that died.

Not all our nests are so eccentric – a hen pheasant found flowers hard to resist and made her nest in a mass of tulips, whilst a pair of nuthatches reared five young in a cavity in a stone wall by our front gate, completely unperturbed by the constant banging and jarring that occurred each time someone came or went. They appeared remarkably tame and still continue to delight us all through the winter.

Nuthatch with food for her young family.

LEFT: *Hen pheasant nesting in tulips.*

BELOW LEFT: *Young great tits nest under a flower pot.*

BELOW RIGHT: *Blue tit feeding young.*

Flycatcher at nest on home-made box.

A load of hay

ONE BEAUTIFUL MORNING in early May, after taking my two labradors for their usual run through birch woods bursting with green, fresh as an ocean breeze, I called to collect our morning papers at the village shop. There I was told that one of my neighbours had been trying to telephone me as a swarm of bees he thought might be mine, had settled near the Manor House. Was I interested and would I take the swarm?

Having recently painted one of my old hives ready for just such an event, I dashed off to take a quick look and assess the situation, meeting my neighbour in the process. He, having failed to catch me at home, had telephoned another bee-keeper. My appearance, however, extracted the promise of a further telephone call to say that his services would not be required after all.

The swarm had formed at the end of a dead branch of a poplar in a hedge, at a height of about 8 feet from the ground, and had arrived there the previous evening.

I have been a very amateur bee-keeper for about twenty-three years, when at our previous home in East Sussex we started a peach orchard with rather more enthusiasm than sense. Having gone quite peachless for several years, we thought – despite being assured that peaches are self fertile – that a hive of bees might help. Good fortune at that time had provided a bee-master of the highest standing who lived only three miles away. He not only supplied the hive and its contents but, far more important as far as we were concerned, looked after it as well – for we had always shown all bees the most healthy respect. All went well for three years, with a growing amount of honey, but still no peaches, when that spring, my bee-master broke the news that his business was being swallowed up by the Crawley development and announced his retirement from the scene.

He promised, however, to show me how to set about my bee requirements with an assurance of its simplicity – adding as an afterthought – many bee-keepers are women, why didn't I ask my wife if she would like the job. I already had, I said, and here I was waiting for my first instruction!

The bee-keepers calendar really starts in April with the spring cleaning of the hive, so with interest overcoming caution, I watched at as discreet a

OPPOSITE
20,000 bees or more!

Dislodging the swarm – one hefty bang!

distance as possible, whilst he set about it. He was, of course, quite immune to bee stings and wore neither veil nor gloves, rather indeed rolling back his shirt sleeves as he warmed to the job. I believe if it had been hot enough he would have thought nothing of stripping to the waist! Feeling it would have been cowardly not to follow suit – omitting the sleeve part – I watched as he opened up the hive, took it apart, scrubbed the floor with carbolic soap, found the queen and saw that all was well. But half way through these proceedings a number of bees, whose behaviour up till then had been remarkably docile – a fact which encouraged me to move closer – began to congregate around my head and neck. Their gentle buzzing changed pitch to one of anger and I was forced to a precipitate, painful and undignified retreat to the house to don veil and gloves – they had apparently taken a marked dislike to my hair oil!

Now a swarm of bees, at any rate when it first leaves the hive, is generally in a most benevolent mood. This is because bees, before swarming, eat as much honey as they can to sustain themselves until they find a new home. The longer they take to do this, the hungrier they become, the more brittle their temperament.

I have over the years taken a number of swarms without undue difficulty. This was because my bees were thoughtful enough to land on a convenient spot – nearly always the lower branch of one of our bush peaches in the orchard – often within a stone's throw of the hive they had just vacated. From the branch they could be easily shaken, boxed and returned at dusk to a new hive.

After the initial swarming scouts fly off in search of a more permanent home – a hollow tree, an old chimney breast or the tiled roof of an old house, even an unoccupied hive – and as soon as they convey their discovery to the swarm, it departs in a brown cloud on buzzing wings. This may happen in a few hours or, in extreme cases, it may take two or three days, so it is important to act at once for there is no telling when they will depart.

Pondering this over a very hurried breakfast, I realised it had been many years since I had taken a swarm – for when we moved to West Sussex I reduced my bee-capade from seven to two hives. I had also become allergic

A new brood chamber houses the swarm – provided the queen goes in.

A swarm of bees on a branch of peach tree.

to bee stings, not immune as might have been expected, so it was with a degree of trepidation I returned to the scene, equipped with all the impedimenta under the sun.

I need not have worried – for the second time that morning the telephone message had failed to get through, and my bee-keeper neighbour was already on the job, spurred on undoubtedly by the old country saying that 'a swarm in May was worth a load of hay' and bees too have kept up with current inflation!

The pictures tell the story, a model operation, not surprising perhaps, as I learned later this well-behaved congregation had come from a church about one and a half miles away.

The bush telegraph

ONE OF THE MANY DELIGHTS of spring is the sight of the first swallows sitting on the telegraph wires that run down the lane, resting after their long flight from Africa, a sight repeated up and down the country. It is a perch they will use on and off throughout the ensuing six months, culminating in a great get-together of families and relations as they mass before leaving our shores. House martins, which are more gregarious, will follow suit in even greater numbers.

I find it fascinating to see so many other birds using the telegraph and power lines wherever they are found, for resting, preening, as a lookout post and even for singing and communicating.

Swallows congregating for the long flight to Africa.

ABOVE: *One of our spotted flycatchers on his favourite perch.*

LEFT: *Cock kestrel eyeing the bank and road for food.*

During the summer months the telegraph wires in our west Sussex lane play host to a pair of little owls that spend much of their time eyeing the road and its verges for food – in their case mostly insects – which are attracted to the warm road surface. A resident kestrel uses the wires for much the same purpose throughout the year, except that voles and mice form its staple diet. In late spring and summer a pair of spotted flycatchers are particularly fond of using the single wire that runs from the telegraph pole across the road to the house. It forms a most convenient perch from which to make endless forays catching all manner of flies and other insects to feed themselves and their young. Had it not been there I think we would have put one up, as their aerobatics give such pleasure.

Winter months bring other sights, flocks of chaffinches and greenfinches, a family of yellow hammers and, in October, a mass of migratory meadow pipits. In late March there is the splendid sight of no less than forty-five goldfinches strung out like rubies on a power line that crosses a nearby field. A flock of goldfinches goes by the delightful name of a 'charm'. What could be more apt?

Starlings, of course, are always around and sometimes gather in vast numbers. Birds reaction to cars is interesting. Some fly off at their approach but the little owls and kestrel nearly always remain unmoved unless I try to stop right underneath them. As long as I keep going, even though at a crawl, they will generally accept that they will come to no harm, so that I become what could truly be called a birds-eye view.

Telegraph wires have a hidden bonus too, for those birds which use them. On busy roads or narrow lanes, the birds fly off at a safe height, well clear of speeding cars and the terrible toll these take on other birds – especially pheasants, too big or unadapted to use them.

A cock yellowhammer at its serenade post.

The water vole

BRIGHT BEADY EYES peered out of reddish brown fur as the water vole sat munching weeds that had caught against posts, creating a miniature log jam. Occasionally he would stop eating and brush his face and whiskers by bringing both paws back over his head simultaneously, then, satisfied there was no danger at hand, he helped himself to another succulent weed. Presently two ponies came by and with a slight plop he dived beneath the surface to swim unseen to one of the underwater entrances to his home in the river bank.

Strictly vegetarian and with very poor eyesight he had allowed me to creep right up to within fourteen feet of where he was feeding. I watched, fascinated with thoughts of Ratty of *Wind in the Willows* fame – 'like the good little fellow he was!' In no way to be confused with the horrible hoards of disease-carrying brown rats that plague our cities and farms and which often take to the fields in summer.

My particular water vole had his home on the Wiltshire Avon, but they are also found on many waterways throughout the country.

Water voles have many enemies, but for once man is not one of them. They really have enough enemies without him. The advent of mink in any area has proved deadly; they can have no escape from these murderous animals by either land or water. Whole populations have been wiped out and have no chance of making a comeback whilst mink remain, and this applies to so much other wildlife. Stoats, weasels, herons and large pike, where these exist, all make life an added danger. Fishing the Tay recently, a ghillie who had spent his life there recalled how, as a boy, he could walk along the bank during the spring and find a moorhen's nest every four hundred yards or so. Now, he said, I can walk four miles without finding one – due entirely to the presence of mink.

In Scotland water voles have black fur and are certainly no less attractive for that. Slightly smaller than their English counterpart and classified as a sub-species, they are found burrowing the banks of many hill lochs and burns. They are never far away from water and are particularly fond of any rush-covered marshy area which provides food and cover from their enemies – the short-eared owl having replaced the barn owl on the moors in this respect.

On the alert. The water vole has poor eyesight and, with no webbed feet, is not a particularly good swimmer.

Years ago, one August Sunday, we were out for a walk along a river in south-west Perthshire when we surprised a young family of water voles – they can only have been a few weeks old and a quarter grown. In adventurous spirit, perhaps not realising their limitations, they had strayed further away from the water than was safe for them. I remember catching one in my hands with the intention of returning it to relative safety when I received a nasty nip in the thumb for my pains. In fact we probably saved at least one of their lives as a buzzard had flown off just before we arrived, and his presence there I am sure was more than just by chance. These voles were only 50 feet above sea level, but up in the hills whole colonies live at heights well over 2,000 feet and must of necessity hibernate during any extremely cold spell when everything is covered with ice and snow. A mild spell soon makes them active again.

It is perhaps interesting to note that, although so dependent on waterways, rivers and lochs, they have not evolved to the extent of having webbed feet and so are not particularly good swimmers. But they can dive and swim well enough under water in an emergency. It would indeed be a sad day if these delightful little creatures were to disappear from the scene for ever – but mink we can do without!

A brush with a cub

TUBBY WAS EXACTLY two days old when he was quite literally snatched from the jaws of death – for Tubby was a hill fox cub. Let me explain.

It is a part of the Highland scene that the hill fox has to be kept within bounds, for they are the scourge of the hill farmer, and lethal predators of both lambs and game. This is fact, not fiction. That they are at the same time beautiful animals only adds a degree of poignancy to their destruction. So it was that one April when the fox hunting season starts in earnest in the highlands, that terriers entered a shallow earth, over 1800 ft, up on the hill where a vixen had recently given birth to cubs, and succeeded after an underground fight in killing the vixen and her cubs. All her cubs that is save one. For when it was all over, the keeper whose name was Davie made one final examination of the scene, and stretching his arm as far as possible into the earth, felt something furry and warm, and came up with one cub quite remarkably unscathed.

Now in 99.9 per cent of these occasions that would have been that so far as the cub was concerned, but for some reason not really clear he tucked the two-day-old into his inside pocket and took it home. Christened Tubby, it received the most caring attention not only by Davie, but by his wife and two daughters, who fed it every few hours for the first ten days with milk through the rubber end of an eye-dropper.

As time progressed it grew up to romp with the very terriers that would normally have torn it to bits, for it seemed its wild smell had been subtly changed by its surroundings and it was accepted as one of them.

Brought into the cottage when quite small, he very soon became completely housetrained, learning this necessity more speedily than most puppies and, rather surprisingly, he did not cause havoc by chewing everything in sight. My young labradors found pretty well everything within reach fair game including a most expensive pair of shoes – my wife's of course – for well over two years.

Tubby now spent most of the day in an enclosure on the lawn with a large wooden box for shelter. When fed he would leave his bowl untouched, watching it like a hawk from the cover of his box in the hope of pouncing

Tubby at seven weeks.

XYL

on any of the local bird population that might be tempted to steal a few crumbs from the dish. As he grew older still, Tubby, whose name had become a bit of a misnomer, used to love the warmth of the living room fire and the comfort of the sofa top. But he was always wary of anyone he did not know, especially as he grew to full maturity.

By then his kennel, like the Labrador's alongside, consisted of a large straw-filled barrel lying on its side, a warm, rain and windproof home; his run, a length of wire between kennel and post. His collar, like any dog, had a chain lead attached to the wire to allow him free access to exercise without giving him complete freedom – that at least was the intention – and, of course, by December Tubby was full grown. In so many similar cases where a fox has become domesticated, the mating season and the call of the wild prove irresistible, and Tubby, being by now the most handsome dog fox, was no exception. Although no one saw him go, he managed to snap a weak link in his lead and disappeared into the night. Five days later he came back none the worse for his exploits.

A few days later he vanished again and this time did not return. He may have been seen in May near the Lodge, for a fox was observed briefly which took little notice of humans. Fortunately he was never bolted by terriers from earth or cairn when fox hunting began again in April, for it would have been a bitter moment had he been shot then. But it seems he was lucky. Had I been out with a gun when he surfaced I am sure I would have looked the other way and I would not have blamed Davie for doing likewise. The affection and care built up over the months is, I think you will agree, self evident from the photographs.

OPPOSITE
Tubby aged eight months.

A foxy epilogue

One mid-November morning I glanced out of the window before dressing to see what the day held in store. It was one of those typical rather dull mornings that one can never be sure will lead to sunshine or rain. A cock and three hen pheasants were feeding on a flower bed; nothing particularly unusual about that as our garden has always been a sanctuary to most bird life, bordering as it does wood and farmland. I was on the point of turning away when all four pheasants heads went up, instantly alert. They can't have seen me, I thought, and sure enough round the corner of the house trotted a fox. They never moved as he jogged towards, but not exactly at, them, but when level and some eight feet away from the cock bird, the fox did a little rugger swerve and a playful snarl before passing on his way. The cock reacted with a couple of quick side-steps to keep a safe distance, and with danger passed, he and the hens resumed feeding. How they knew they were not on the menu for breakfast I have no idea, but know they certainly did. It was a fascinating way to start a dull November day!

Myth and legend surround the fox as it does few other animals, often with an extraordinary cloak of sentimentality. That it is a creature of great beauty few will deny, but alas its killer instincts bring it into direct conflict with man.

Sentimentality is often misplaced but there is one delightful true story I must mention of a friend who inadvertently allowed a very young terrier puppy to stray too near an earth containing fox cubs. The vixen rushed out of the bushes and knocked the pup over, probably fully intending to kill it, which she could easily have done in a second. But her maternal instincts would not let her do it; she realised that the pup was a baby and, instead of biting, she just held it down with her paws. As my friend shouted and ran, she made off into the bushes again, turning to glance out once more and disappeared. This bit of chivalry impressed him very much, and he resolved to be as fair as possible in his dealings with foxes in the future.

Recounting this to one of our farming neighbours, he told me of one occasion when he sent his dog, a young labrador after a fox as it was trotting across an open field in broad daylight. His dog had a fair turn of speed, and caught up with the fox which turned, instead of running off, and proceeded to rub noses with it!

This behaviour reminded me of the unique film made in the Hudson Bay area of Canada, which millions saw on their television screens some months ago, of a husky tethered in the snow by a length of chain jumping up and down with excitement as a Polar Bear lumbered towards it. To our amazement instead of making a quick meal of the dog, they proceeded to play with each other in the most friendly and energetic fashion!

Caught mousing in the heather and sniffing at every tussock in the process.

SUMMER

But green leaves and blossoms and sunny warm weather,

And singing and loving – all come together.

But the lark is so brimful of gladness and love,

The green fields below him, the blue sky above

That he sings, and he sings; and forever sings he –

'I love my Love and my Love loves me!'

COLERIDGE: *Answer to a child's question.*

Incredible journeys

I NEVER THINK SUMMER has really arrived until our spotted flycatchers are sitting safely on their eggs below our bedroom window. There's something strangely reassuring about their arrival and to know they have made the trip all the way back from Africa safely. And although one swallow doesn't make a summer their return from several thousand miles is for me nothing less than miraculous – as is all migration.

For just as spring visitors arrive from the south, so will our winter migrants be winging it north to feed and breed in the almost continuous daylight of a northern summer, before making the return trip with their young a few months later. Some, like the Arctic tern, make quite incredible journeys an almost non-stop affair as they circumnavigate the globe, nesting in Iceland and other northern regions, then with their young, follow the sun and overwinter in the Antarctic, before returning to the same spot to nest again the following spring – a round trip of not less than 22,000 miles!

OPPOSITE
Red admiral feeding on a bird-pecked apple.

RIGHT
Spotted flycatcher – ever on the alert for insects.

Equally incredible, if not more so, was the case of a Manx shearwater taken from its nesting site off the Pembrokeshire coast, carried by air to Boston and released near the international airport, with only the sea between its release point and nesting site. Twelve and a half days later it was back at its nest, a flight of well over 3,000 miles. No landmarks, only the ocean waves to guide it!

Whilst bird migration must rank as one of the many wonders of this world, butterfly migration is for me even more remarkable. A few years ago we were in Majorca in April. In the north of the island painted lady butterflies were everywhere. When we got home the garden and surrounding fields and woods were soon alive with them, and by mid-June quite a few had reached the north-east of Scotland.

A monarch butterfly feeding on Solidago *– a golden rod – photographed near Cape Cod.*

A painted lady and other insects feeding on sedum.

Casting back through old reports showed that over 100 years ago, in 1879, the largest migration of painted ladies occurred when a swarm of these butterflies left North Africa in such colossal numbers they cast a shadow on the ground. Even this paled by comparison with the migration of monarch butterflies that takes place regularly every year in America. In 1885 a flight of these butterflies in New Jersey was described as 'almost beyond belief, millions is but feeble expression, miles of them no exaggeration!'

Reflect for a moment on the difference between birds and insects, for the individual butterfly the journey is almost always one way. Monarch

butterflies, which we now know come from Canada and the United States east of the Rockies, migrate year after year to the same trees in the 10,000 ft high mountains not all that far from Mexico City. There they rest by the hundreds of thousands. This is a feat of navigation beyond our comprehension, for it excludes all possibility of memory. Last year's insects are not the same as this year's, nor have they any kind of family connection between mother and young which would allow learning of the route to take place.

What happens is this. Only one of the three to six generations of butterflies born each year in Canada and America actually migrates south to Mexico. Those born during the height of summer simply emerge, disperse, breed and die within four to five weeks. Those that are transformed from caterpillars to butterflies in early September somehow know, perhaps by the length of days or some built-in instinct, not to mate. Instead they feed for all they are worth on nectar-laden flowers to fatten themselves so as to have enough energy for the long migration and subsequent winter's rest. Apparently the mountains provide the right temperature for they become almost dormant, living off their fat as do many hibernating animals. They don't eat but must have water and the forest provides this. With the end of winter, when the sun warms them back to full life, they mate and lay their eggs on milkweed on their way back north. A few generations later and back they come on their southern migration. Surely this must be one of Nature's most incredible journeys.

How do the monarchs – and birds – navigate on their long journeys? One recent hypothesis is that they are equipped with a magnetic compass – and in the case of monarchs – with a genetic program that enables them to follow small variations in the Earth's magnetic field. They may also – as birds must – navigate by the sun. It is a sense that man himself has long since lost and I doubt he ever had it save perhaps on a much reduced scale in the Aboriginals of Australia, Eskimos of the Arctic and Bushmen of Africa.

So the next time you see a painted lady on your buddleia or sedum or a red admiral sipping his fill in your orchard from some rotten apple or plum, spare a thought for that incredible journey they made to get there.

But I would not like the reader to assume that every painted lady and red admiral seen is necessarily a migrant. It may well be that many will be home bred from migrants which arrived in late spring or summer. Migratory specimens, however, will continue to arrive well into September, especially in fine sunny weather.

OPPOSITE
A young cuckoo, fostered probably by a hedge sparrow, will soon be flying solo to its winter haunts in southern Africa; with no parents to guide it, an incredible journey of many thousand miles.

Woodpeckers – friend and foe!

GREEN WOODPECKERS in our part of the world – West Sussex – seem to be on the up and up. Wherever I walk in the surrounding woods and birch common I am greeted by their yaffle, that melodious call described by Gilbert White 'as a sort of loud and hearty laugh', from which it takes its popular country name. As a boy I was told that when you hear its call, rain was is the way. Now, the end of August, how we wish that was true after months of drought!

Throughout the winter and spring a pair visited our lawn for leather jackets, cockchafer and other grubs, and this summer have brought their young to eat the ants that nest between the flagstones and on the lawn itself. Now with the ground rock hard, they still manage to find food that other birds cannot reach.

Although we hang up fat and peanuts throughout the winter months they have not yet favoured us with a visit – unlike their relative the great spotted woodpecker which is in constant attendance whenever such food is on offer – but I gather that the green woodpecker in some areas has learnt to come. The great spotted woodpecker is a remarkably handsome and relatively common bird, and there can be few country gardens with a peanut feeder on hand that does not entice them.

Both woodpeckers are beautiful and in their strikingly different colours it would be hard to say which is the more so.

Two season ago, after our spotted flycatchers had arrived in May, and had started to build their nest on the wall opposite our house in a special box provided, we were horrified to see it attacked by a great spotted woodpecker which ripped most of the nesting material out, despite valiant protest from both parent flycatchers. A tap or two on the window scared the marauder away, and to our amazement and delight, the pair of flycatchers immediately set about repairing the havoc that very day, and laid four eggs in the days that followed. The big question then was how to avert another attack, so having already stopped feeding peanuts, I immediately refilled the feeders and kept them going throughout the remaining weeks of May to the

Young green woodpecker after ants, one of its favourite foods.

end of June. Not only did this have the desired effect, for the flycatchers successfully reared four young, but gave us an enthralling sight of three young great spotted woodpeckers coming to our peanuts and being fed by their parents. It is a fact that great spotted woodpeckers will attack other bird's nests. One of our neighbours experienced the destruction of a brood of blue tits from a nest box he had hung from his house, whilst a green woodpecker has been known to kill a fledgling thrush. They are, like so many wild things, beasts as well as beauties.

The lesser spotted woodpecker, about half the size of the great spotted woodpecker, is much less common and a shy bird. It prefers the peace and quiet of the surrounding woods, especially those with standing dead trees from which they can extract woodlice and other grubs that are found in decaying timber.

All woodpeckers have a most distinctive dipping flight like the swing of a pendulum and all three species drum, though the green woodpecker seldom does it. This has been doubted, but evidence is supplied by several authorities on the subject. However, there is no mistaking the drumming of the great spotted woodpecker as it hammers its beak on a dead branch, ten strokes to the second. It is for me one of the most evocative notes of spring, and almost as exciting as the sight of the first swallow.

OPPOSITE
Young great spotted woodpecker being fed by its parent.

RIGHT
Adult green woodpecker.

Little deer

I HAVE FISHED many rivers with friends, guides and ghillies, but only once, in the Scottish Highlands, has my companion been a roe deer! This delightful animal, orphaned when very young, had been rescued and hand reared by a shepherd after its mother had been killed on the road, and in due course was allowed free rein to return to the wild. That the wild happened to be an area adjoining one of the best pools on the river, lying close to the farm where it had spent its very early days, was fortuitous and this three-month-old fawn seldom missed the opportunity to join in the fun whenever anyone was fishing there. Indeed it was so tame it would feed from your hand, and at times would almost trip you up, so closely did it follow proceedings. Very much the opposite of the shy wild roe that lived in the woods up and down the glen, for along with red deer, they are true natives, and have inhabited the Highlands long before man.

OPPOSITE
A magnificent roe buck already in his summer coat, taken in mid-April.

BELOW
Roe deer and fawn.

Reintroduced to the south at the end of the last century, they have spread out to a remarkable degree, as many gardeners with unfenced rose beds will have learnt to their cost for, along with brambles, roses are a favourite delicacy. One year recently, a doe and her twins managed to get access to our kitchen garden whilst we were away, by the simple expedient of jumping a four-foot gate. Why they had never thought of doing this before was a bit of a puzzle, for the gate had been there for at least fifteen years. They helped themselves to one or two rows of maturing lettuce, one crunchy mouthful after another, and four rows of broad beans plus some well advanced runners. My eldest son, down for the weekend, disturbed them in the process, and saw them jump out over the gate in fine style, but left it at that. So, when all was quiet, they simply returned to finish their meal at leisure. There was very little left when we returned a few days later! We love our roe deer but this was trying us to the full. Of course it had been entirely my fault, and another two foot was immediately added to the gate – which would have saved the problem in the first place. Outside the kitchen garden a small orchard of Victoria plums and greengages borders with field and wood, and unfenced, has produced splendid crops for years. The lower branches are sometimes nibbled by roe deer, but surprisingly they do not help themselves to the plums even when ripe.

One summer the field opposite produced a splendid crop of wheat. Whether our local resident roe had heard about the EEC grain mountain I know not, but one sunny morning we found a doe obviously doing its bit to reduce the surplus!

Helping to reduce the grain mountain!

During the rutt, which takes place from mid-July to the end of August, the buck often chases the doe round in circles, forming quite well defined tracks known as roe rings. Unlike red and fallow deer, roe live in family groups, and during the summer months have the richest bright chestnut red coats, which in winter turn to much thicker coats of dark greyish brown.

Although not popular with foresters, because it can undoubtedly do much damage to young plantations – the buck stripping the bark with its exceedingly sharp tines, as well as eating tender young shoots – it is now well established as part of the country scene. I for one would in no way want it otherwise.

My Scottish Highlands fishing companion accepting a tit-bit from 'Aunt' Ness.

Midsummer nightjars

'THE NIGHTJARS ARE BACK,' I said, as I returned from our nearby common, an undulating area of birch and bracken, after taking Sally, my black Labrador, for her evening constitutional.

It was the third week of May and their churring greeting was as welcome a sound to hear as the sight of the first swallow. Nightjars have been with us for many years, and it is always good to know they have come back from their African winter haunts safely, to nest with us again.

That first evening they had flown over and around us in that gliding, lilting flight, like thistledown carried on the wind, hawking for the many moths and other insects that abound in the area. They were quite undisturbed by our presence, their churring call rising and falling as they changed direction or drifted effortless in and out of our hearing.

Noted for their curiosity, it seemed as the season progressed that Sally and I had to be inspected each evening when we ventured out at dusk, often at remarkable close quarters. The cock bird in particular seemed to delight in a close inspection, sometimes hovering above us like a kestrel, and at times I thought he would land on my head. To Sally he paid less attention but would occasionally land in the ride in front of her to seize some insect as an hors-d'oeuvre before departing in search of the main course. Once we got to know each other I would find him sitting on top of a dead sapling birch, his favourite lookout post, but as always he would fly over to inspect us and say good evening. By the end of June the churring became less frequent, often replaced by a chattering call – perhaps we had ventured too close to their nest – and a 'clap' of wings above Sally's head, a warning not to venture any further. This 'clap', rather louder than the noise of a woodpigeon suddenly breaking cover, is made I believe by a sudden wing movement trapping air between wing and body, not as some think by their wings beating against each other.

We never looked for their nest – they have none as such, just a scrape in the ground – for I had no desire to disturb them. But I doubt we would have found it anyway, as a nightjar's plumage melts so perfectly in to the dead leaves and bracken when 'sitting' or at roost and, to complete the deception, it goes one better than most birds by closing its eyes as well. Even sitting on the branch of a tree they are incredibly hard to see.

These warm midsummer evenings bring other bonuses with the serenity of departing day. A spark glows amongst the bracken – bright as a 3-carat diamond, a real live spark, but not from any fire – it is a glow-worm whose lantern shines so brightly and whose life history was portrayed so delightfully many years ago by Henri Farbe.

It is the female who glows so brightly and continues to glow even when I pick her up. They are not numerous. We may only find seven or eight, at most a dozen, in the course of our walk, for there are relatively few snails in our area on which they feed.

Of course the glow-worm is no worm but a beetle, the female never maturing beyond the larval stage, but even the eggs she lays glow if dug up.

Henri Farbe's enquiring mind spurred him to make intricate experiments into the whys and wherefores of these fascinating creatures. What had made their light glow, why females kept their lanterns glowing strongly, whilst males with weaker lamps doused their light at the sound of a footfall – when females were undaunted by a shower of water or a gun fired close to their cage. Only his pipe smoke choked them off – and then only for a flickering moment.

Years pass quickly and the hurricane of October 1987 devastated a huge area of the south. Our common did not escape its ravages, and it seems our nightjars have found another home, for we no longer hear that unique churring call that signals their arrival in May. But the glow-worms are still with us. Perhaps their lanterns will one day guide them back.

OPPOSITE
A male nightjar comes over to say good-evening – taken with a normal lens and flash, which did not disburb it in the least!

The year of the purple emperor

I RATHER LIKE the Chinese habit of naming the year after an animal – let's say the Year of the Pig. If I follow this through in my own way, whilst 1976 would undoubtedly have been named the Year of the Ladybird, 1984 would for us have been called the Year of the Purple Emperor. These two years were in complete contrast, for whereas millions of ladybirds appeared that July – the like of which had seldom if ever been seen before – our purple emperors numbered exactly two – a male and a female,

Although living in a part of West Sussex where purple emperors are not as rare as elsewhere in the south, for over 20 years, I had never seen one in our garden. Perhaps we had been unlucky or unobservant, for one of our friends who lived in the wooded hills two miles away is regularly visited each year by one or two which invade her kitchen. The fact that they are lovers of rotten meat and other disagreeable morsels should not be taken as a slur on her culinary activities!

Male purple emperor, with wings closed, feeding on dung.

A perfect male displaying its beautiful purple sheen.

I came across our male purple emperor quite by chance at the edge of our wood, feeding intently on partially rotted dung one Sunday morning in late July. The wonderful summer had already brought more than the usual sighting of white admirals, and in the spring far more orange tips and brimstones than for years past, whilst one of our near neighbour's gardens in July was alive with silver-washed frittilaries and peacocks – I have never seen so many – and they had seen three purple emperors too. Our own male purple emperor was an absolutely perfect specimen – it cannot have been long hatched – and thinking I must at all costs record the event on film I rushed back to the house to get my camera. Starting to photograph it from a respectable distance, I gradually worked closer so as not to lose the opportunity of some sort of photographic record of such a rare visitor. As things turned out, I need not have worried for to my amazement it allowed me to close the distance to some 18 inches, so intent was it on its morning meal. By this time almost my whole family, including two grandchildren, had gathered round to watch whilst I switched from negative colour film to positive, and it was at this juncture that our purple emperor closed his wings and stubbornly refused to open them. He had co-operated so remarkably well when I had first spotted him feeding with wings open, but now, as I waited crouched for over twenty minutes within two feet of him, he maintained his stance with wings firmly folded and thus without revealing his beautiful purple sheen. I knew any sudden action might frighten him away for good, so very cautiously I tried shading the sun from him with my hand and passing it back and forth, without getting any reaction. I clapped my hands together three feet above him – still no reaction! I shouted – the same result! Then, in desperation, I lowered my hand very slowly towards him, and with one finger very gently touched the tip of his closed wings – a momentary flicker was the only response! I repeated the performance twice more before it finally proved too much even for him, and he flew off to settle on a maple some ten yards away – with wings open, but out of reach of me and my camera. Five minutes later he was back. Had I attempted any of these ploys with almost any other butterfly it would have been off like a shot. I recounted all this to our neighbour who told me one had come into his sitting- room, landed on his arm, walked down it and all over his hand!

It is, of course, the male purple emperor only which is endowed with beautiful purple sheen and which gives the butterfly its name, for the female is a drab black and white. Little did we think we should be fortunate enough to see a female of the species as well, but exactly two weeks later, out walking in the afternoon, we found a female sunning herself on a clump of ivy next to a number of sallow trees on which she lays her eggs – one at a time as a rule and dispersed over a wide area. This specimen was rather the worse for wear, having a large portion of her lower wing missing, but she flew well enough, though no great distance, when finally disturbed – and being August she had hopefully completed her egg-laying activities to produce a bumper crop of purple emperors next year.

Moths of the summer night – and day

THE MAJORITY OF COUNTRY DWELLERS hardly notice the enormous number and variety of moths living on their doorsteps. Because, by and large, moths are nocturnal in habit, this is hardly surprising. But occasionally some unusual specimen will fly in through an open window after dark, drawn by the light inside and, more often than not when this happens, it is considered an unwelcome guest and linked with such noxious visitors as cockchafers and other 'things that go bump in the night'.

Caterpillars are a different proposition. Nearly all garden plants from roses to raspberries provide food for one kind or another, and woolly bears – the hawk-moth caterpillars with their distinctive horned tails – stick caterpillars and many others are known to most countrymen. Unfortunately, many moths are undoubted pests to farmers and gardeners, but I must confess I hate the thought of eyed hawk-moth caterpillars forcibly drinking nicotine or sulphur sprays when these are applied to the apple orchard. Luckily, by no means all moths do harm, whilst others such as the gaudy garden tiger certainly cannot be faulted for choosing a nettlebed on which to feed.

Day-flying scarlet tiger moths mating on leaf of a comfrey plant.

Five-spot burnets feeding on a thistle.

I first started my collection many years ago, passing through the schoolboy stage of bug hunting and caterpillar collecting. My efforts were lighthearted, and during several years in which my interest grew, I succeeded in amassing an indifferent case or two of common varieties. With the war years intervening, my amateur collection grew paler and more bedraggled and, although my interest never completely deserted me, it certainly lay dormant.

I think it was a visit to the south of France during the summer of 1955 which really rekindled this interest, for on our first evening there, with the Mediterranean below us, we sat on a floodlit balcony backed by mimosa trees with other hotel guests, sipping our coffee and generally relaxing in the warm night air. A large moth spiralled down towards me from the trees above, and in less time than it takes to tell I whipped out my handkerchief and made a wild and unsuccessful grab at it, chasing it in my enthusiasm at floor level under my neighbour's chair. Finally coming up with it safely in my grasp, I dashed off to dispose of it in the quiet sanctity of my room. By

Two peppered moths. The top picture shows a moth which has adapted to industrial pollution.

then, of course, the whole hotel assumed a madman was in their midst.

My calmer return some minutes later and the revelation of a striped hawk-moth was greeted more broadmindedly than I had dared hope, and for the next few days the hunt was on, aided and abetted in no small way by many of those present. In fact, I think only our waiter continued to doubt my sanity, believing that we were bent on eating our catch. On reflection, however, it is more probable that his was the gourmet's passion and he looked upon me as a poacher.

I have often wondered what our moth trap would have attracted had I owned one then, but shortly after my return I heard that there were such things and, like a father wanting a good excuse to play trains, I decided that my eldest son should have one for Christmas. It has given us all immense pleasure ever since.

It is large and similar in principle to a fish trap. The base is about 2ft in diameter, and is little more than a circular tin, on top of which sits a transparent cone of celluloid. This tapers upwards to hold a finned lamp holder through which moths fly inside when attracted by the light. The special mercury-vapour electric bulb gives out a dazzling, bluish-white glow which has a tremendous area of attraction – on a dark night moths will fly from distances of up to half a mile, conceivably more.

Not all moths are drawn to light, and of those that are, by no means all will enter the trap. In the morning, if the light is left on throughout the night, many moths will be found in the surrounding grass. Unless you wish the local bird population to enjoy a good breakfast, an early rise is essential. Failure to do this will reveal a sorrowful pattern of disaster and perhaps the wing of a most sought-after species, the sole clue to its presence. Bats, too, can be a nuisance once they know the form. The trap does not, of course, kill the insects, but care must be taken to put some loose egg trays or wrinkled paper in the base so that moths entering will crawl under them for shade and not flutter too much, because then they might damage their wings.

Our most successful hauls have generally been on moonless nights, and a night of soft, warm rain does not reduce the yield at all. Cold nights or windy ones are bad. Our rarest catches have so far been a bedstraw hawk-moth taken in July and a really magnificent specimen of a death's-head hawk-moth which was found about teatime in September on the wall of our house, where it had flown to roost – undoubtedly drawn by the light which had been on all the night before.

Examining the nights' catch in the trap.

There is little point in using the trap every night, because some nights will be quite unsuitable, but by using it at regularly spaced intervals one is able to obtain a good cross-section of the local moths and to learn much about them. If trapping can perhaps be criticised as a lazy way of collecting, used sensibly it will, none the less, provide much knowledge and enjoyment. But indiscriminate catching may easily reduce populations of the rarer kinds, so traps should only be used with great discretion and a sense of responsibility.

Hawk-moths, queens of the night

In nature not all living creatures are beautiful or attractive. Some can repel or even frighten. Few people are attracted by spiders and snakes scare me stiff. Yet among the vast family of insects it is as if the Almighty had created butterflies and moths simply to give us pleasure, for their beauty, to greater or lesser extent, is beyond question. And of all the species of *lepidoptera* none is more fascinating to me than are the hawk-moths.

One has only to see hawk-moths in flight to understand why they have been given this name. With their long, knife-edged tapering wings and streamlined bodies, they fly incredibly fast, and few who have watched them sucking the nectar can fail to be impressed, as they hover and dart from bloom to bloom.

Almost as fascinating as the moths themselves are their caterpillars with those thick, strong colourful bodies and distinctive horns at the tail. Perhaps people find them more in this form than as moths.

Some years ago on holiday in Corsica towards the end of September, we saw many full-grown convolvulus hawk-moth caterpillars wandering across the road and the toll passing cars took was high. They were searching for a convenient place soft enough to dig down a few inches and pupate, as do all hawk-moth caterpillars. There they overwinter before hatching out as adult moths in late spring or summer. In England I have found poplar, privet and elephant hawk-moth caterpillars in the same way, though a search for these and other hawk-moth caterpillars on their favourite food plant is often relatively easy.

On another occasion some years ago, while walking to the beach along a disused weed-covered railway line in the south of France, I found several almost fully grown spurge hawk-moth caterpillars. These have a very striking appearance – bright reddish-brown colouring with white circular, almost luminous, large and much smaller markings down their sides – and proved the centre of attraction that evening when exhibited in a toothmug in the bar, feeding on long sprays of spurge.

A privet hawk-moth shows off its beautiful shape and colour, and streamlined body.

When a day or so later we went out to gather some fresh spurge for them, we discovered some younger spurge hawk-moth caterpillars, and just before our departure, while the first were going to ground, we found some that can only have been hatched a few days. Of three pupae which I brought home, two stayed in this form for two years before emerging as perfect moths.

Of the 27 different varieties of hawk-moths found in Europe, one-third are natives of Britain and another third either reach us as migrants or wander here by chance on extremely irregular visits. No one knows why they come, for, unlike most migrants who do so for food, few have much chance of breeding successfully. The death's head hawk-moth pupa is unlikely to withstand our winter even if its caterpillar survived the risk of being sprayed to death on the potato leaves on which it feeds.

The oleander hawk-moth, a moth of great beauty and an extreme rarity, would be clever to find a suitable food plant on which to deposit its eggs. But one was successful many years ago in its quest, for two oleander hawk-moth caterpillars were found on an oleander in a derelict greenhouse in the Midlands. By uncanny instinct it was guided to the oleander; I refuse to think that it was just luck. The discovery of any of these migratory moths in one's garden is always an event and, over the years, two bedstraw, a convolvulus, spurge and a monster death's head have come our way.

In 'hawk-moth years' vast numbers are found over the whole country, but more particularly in the south. A vintage year for the death's head hawk-moths was 1956, when tremendous numbers were to be seen all over Britain. The first wave arrived around mid-summer, but the largest influx took place that September. One particular event was reported in the news-

Our death's head hawk-moth (actual size).

A humming bird hawk-moth taking nectar from a zinnia in Majorca. It is a not uncommon migrant to Britain.

papers. A yachtsman, navigating one foggy night in the English Channel off Dunkirk, noticed his rigging looked rather thick and blurred against the sky, to discover it was covered with a mass of death's head hawk-moths, which all flew off just before dawn.

We found one magnificent specimen then, as big as any I have seen, on the north wall of our house. A mile away another was picked up by the youngest son of a friend – aged five. He understandably dropped it when it squeaked like a mouse, a habit which it now appears indicates an empty stomach – thanks to some research with one of these insects on a honeycomb, carried out by Hugh Newman, and described in his book, *Hawk-moths of Great Britain and Europe*.

Death's heads are not the only hawk-moths to migrate in force. Some years have witnessed a huge influx of such varieties as the striped and bedstraw and, less frequently, the convolvulus, whose whirring flight at dusk is of such speed and power. But by far the commonest migrant is the entrancing little day-flying humming bird hawk-moth, which looks like a

A male emperor moth caterpillar. The male has yellow spots and the female has purple spots. The colours follow through on the wings of the adult insect. Day flying, it is the only British species of silk moth belonging to the Saturnidae *family.*

miniature humming-bird itself. It is a regular annual visitor, sometimes plentiful, and one which is probably seen more and known best because of its diurnal habit. It is also the only one of our hawk-moths to hibernate.

What of our natives? Two of the earliest to appear each summer are the day-flying bee hawk-moths. How many people, I wonder, who may see these fast little insects with their almost transparent wings, simply mistake them for yet another large bumble-bee and pass them by without a second glance.

But my favourite is the privet hawk-moth, a most strikingly handsome and powerful flier, not as highly colourful as some, but beautifully marked with pink-tinged underwings, charcoal-coloured lines and pink-and-black barred body. It is relatively common throughout the country, especially in the south, as are the elephant and small elephant hawks, which many people consider more beautiful. Their name comes from their caterpillar's appearance. We find the elephant hawk-moth in our garden from the beginning of June until the end of July, and sometimes even into early August, for, unlike the lime, eyed and poplar hawks, it feeds on honeysuckle and many other garden and wild sweet-scented flowers. These last three have a much shorter life because their mouths have remained underdeveloped and

OPPOSITE: *Attracted by the light of a mercury vapour bulb, two elephant hawk-moths show off their wonderful protective colouring. They are resting on honeysuckle, a favourite nectar source.*

they cannot feed themselves in the same way. The commonest of all our native hawk-moths is the poplar, an insect which varies considerably in colours. It has a clumsier flight than most hawk-moths, but, like its caterpillar, it is still a most striking insect. When at rest it does not fold its wings close along the length of its body as do the privet and convolvulus hawk-moths and others, but it simulates the bark of a poplar tree with wings overlapping each other, upper wing down, under wing up. Protective colouring is essential to survival when the insect is at rest.

The eyed hawk-moth goes one stage better and attempts to scare its enemies away. Touch one and it will flick its upper wing forward to reveal its rose-coloured under wing with its distinctive and lifelike eye from which it takes its name. The movement is very quick and has been proved to frighten birds which would otherwise gobble it up. I suspect that the reddish marking on the under wing of the poplar hawk is intended for the same purpose.

Hawk-moths take some time to warm up before they fly if they have remained settled for any length of time. This takes the form of vibrating wings at high speed, and is reminiscent of the warming-up of a propeller-driven aeroplane.

A full-grown privet hawk-moth caterpillar. In a few hours or days it will have burrowed underground to pupate and hatch out the following summer.

A spurge hawk-moth caterpillar feeding on the plant from which it takes its name.

A perfect specimen of a lime hawk-moth roosting on a fence in daylight.

A poplar hawk-moth – our commonest hawk-moth – resting on the trunk of a poplar tree.

If the poplar is our commonest hawk-moth, then our rarest is the pine hawk. Ninety years ago it was considered almost non-existent in Britain, but with the advent of increased pine woods it has managed to go against the modern trend in which birds and animals fight for survival, and is now far more common throughout the south of England. At any rate no summer passes without yielding several specimens in our moth trap, an essential investment for all interested in learning about our *lepidoptera*.

Corn circles

CORN CIRCLES sometimes hit the local headlines. They are, after all, often a most impressive and intriguing sight, but the poor farmer on whose land they occur must suffer considerable damage and financial loss.

When in July 1995 I took this photograph near Winchester – and there were two other corn circles nearby – I wrote to a great friend who had been farming most of his life in south-west Scotland and asked him what he knew about them. His reply was to the point – 'we cannot afford to do that up here!'

It is apparently an established fact that they are man made – sometimes – but how does this explanation stand up to the extraordinary occurrence this summer, widely reported, near Stonehenge, where as always there was a crowd of people. At 4 o'clock in the afternoon there was nothing out of the ordinary in the surrounding fields, but just half an hour later, there it was, a huge corn circle, without its implementation being observed. Perhaps it is all best summed up in Shakespeare's *Hamlet* – 'There are more things in Heaven and Earth, Horatio, than are dreamt of in your philosophy!'

The huge corn circle near Winchester.

AUTUMN

There's a whisper down the field where the year has shot her yield
and the ricks stand grey to the sun.
Singing over then, come over, for the bee has quit the clover
and your English summer's done.

KIPLING: *The Long Trail.*

The labrador and the hedgehog

Curls up but can't swim – stickly – prickly, that's him! To all lovers of Kipling's *Just So Stories* these words need no introduction, but Don my golden labrador – whose father, mother, brothers and sisters be it noted were all black – seemed just as perplexed with his first hedgehog as Painted Jaguar.

Indeed his bark was very much worse than his bite when one evening last autumn he returned rather later than usual to the back door carrying one of the largest, fattest hedgehogs I have ever seen. How he picks them up and carries them without harm either to himself or the hedgehog I only witnessed months later. But from September onwards, until hibernation forced their disappearance,he seemed to delight in discovering and retrieving any hedgehog which was foolish enough to wander into the garden from the surrounding fields and hedgerows, dumping them unceremoniously on the lawn at my feet. Then with tail wagging, he would look up at me as if to say 'All right, I can do it, now you try!'

So when a friend telephoned one day in July with the news that he had just lost his complete sitting of bantam eggs that morning and held the culprit captive in his henhouse, I went over armed with camera and Don beside me.

Without really intending he proceeded to get in on the act. First pawing the hedgehog in puzzlement and frowning deeply, he proceeded to grapple with the problem, bending his head on one side then leaning forward he manoeuvred into position for comfort, very carefully opened his mouth and lifted the spiky ball triumphantly upwards. Quite satisfied at having retrieved it successfully he deposited the hedgehog on the lawn where a few minutes later he slowly uncurled and made off unscathed. Indeed so unscathed was he that a week or two later he was up to his usual mischief in the henhouse, this time devouring some day-old chicks. Even this episode only caused his removal from the immediate locality to a wood three miles away where no such succulent morsels existed.

Maybe we shall find him at our own back door one autumn evening. If so it will be a fair bet he won't have made the journey altogether on his own.

Don – triumphant!

Mushrooms for breakfast

Fine specimens of shaggy cap or lawyer's wig.

I RECALL YEARS AGO when space exploration began in earnest, a comment that if any living matter was ever discovered in space it might well prove to be a mushroom spore. Lifted by thermal winds, spore can be carried many thousands of miles, and it is a fact that a Danish handbook on fungi will serve almost equally well for North America – as long as you are a good linguist.

Fungi have existed since the beginning of time, and in Britain alone there are over three thousand varieties. They act as nature's waste disposers, breaking down dead or decaying matter and recycling it. They also take on both beautiful and weird shapes, sizes and colours; though, lacking chlorophyll, green is not one of them.

Many are edible, some quite delicious and a few – about one per cent – downright deadly, so a little knowledge is a very dangerous thing.

Most of us in Britain think in simple terms of mushrooms and toadstools – I know I do – looking at the latter with deep suspicion. But if you lived in Poland or Russia, or for that matter most of Northern Europe, you would find almost three hundred varieties of fungi which can be legally sold. And one really shouldn't restrict it to Northern Europe. For the Romans sent their slaves out in search of edible fungi for festive occasions, and that was almost two thousand years ago. Today, the French relish the chantarelle, and the edible boletus, known on the Continent as cep, is equally prized. Both are quite distinctive and delicious to eat as are several others, but it is not my intention to try and act as a guide book on mushrooms and fungi, for there are some wonderfully illustrated books on the subject.

In Britain, 1990 was a universally marvellous year for field mushrooms, and in the water meadows below us the crop began in mid-September, just after the first rains, after a wonderful summer and we were picking them right the way through until the first frosts of mid-November, an unusually long period. Other parts of the country all reported record crops. The mushrooms picked in 1990 were almost all perfect, those the next year, almost all, however freshly picked, had been attacked by maggots of the mushroom fly and ninety per cent of the crop had to be discarded as a result. Whether this proved the reason for the almost complete absence of

OPPOSITE
Just a few moments work – a delicious trugful of field mushrooms.

RIGHT
Bracket fungi, Piptoporus betulinus, *found on dead or dying birch trees.*

OPPOSITE
TOP LEFT: *orange peel fungus*
TOP RIGHT: *chanterelle*
BOTTOM: *edible boletus, which is known on the Continent as cep.*

RIGHT: *shaggy parasol mushroom.*

mushrooms in 1992 or whether this was from other causes I do not profess to know; they had almost vanished from the scene and I picked only a capful. What I do know is that there is nothing to touch them, picked fresh, with bacon and eggs for breakfast or fried in butter with a juicy steak. They possess a flavour altogether superior to their cultivated kin. The picture of the trug basket tells the story – it took only a few minutes to fill.

OPPOSITE: *The brilliantly coloured – but poisonous – fly agaric,* Amanita muscaria.

RIGHT: *Stump fungus.*

FOR ALL SEASONS

There is only man for all seasons
And in deed he is the one.
He ascends the animal kingdom
And rises like the sun.
He may not be the forebear
Of all that lives and breathes.
From the fish the animals and birds
in flight
He only can bequeath.

Upon his dog he casts his mantle
To nourish and protect.
To walk beside him thro' all seasons
With gun or crook or net.

ANON

The charm of kestrels

IF YOU TRAVEL along one of many motorways for an hour or more, my guess is that you will see at least one kestrel hovering over you during that time. In a recent journey north, before lunch I counted no less than seven and I was driving. My wife, had she not fallen asleep, might well have seen more. The first was on the M25 near Heathrow – unbelievably in the centre of the road between two fast lanes, hovering at about 30 feet. There was little or no grass but there it was. I hope it didn't linger there too long for with four lanes of traffic each way travelling at high speed, it was putting itself at considerable risk, but it must have found it worthwhile or it would not have been there. Further north, with grassy banks to harbour voles, their presence was more understandable, but it was extraordinary how they have adapted to the horrors of, dare I say it, the rat race.

Kestrels are our commonest bird of prey and widespread throughout Great Britain. Instantly distinguishable by their almost unique ability to hover motionless as they scan the ground below, an ability that has earned them the name windhover. They will gradually quarter an area, dropping down a few feet or slipping sideways in the wind to resume their search, before falling like a stone on some unsuspecting mouse, their staple diet.

No other bird of prey hunts in quite the same way, though an osprey will hover momentarily above the water before taking the plunge, and buzzards will hang motionless into the wind, scarcely moving their wings in the process. A kestrel hovering by comparison seems indefatigable and has an identity all its own.

It is remarkable that when a kestrel is hovering near a hedgerow where finches or other small birds are present, the latter will show no alarm and appear to know instinctively they are not the target; a very different reaction to that displayed had a sparrow hawk – much the same size as a kestrel – been in the vicinity.

I recall a friend telling me some years ago of an osprey that stayed on his stretch of river for some weeks. One day he watched it as it too hovered above the water, before plunging down to catch a trout amongst a whole lot of mallard. Their only reaction was to flap their wings excitedly in, as he put it, an aquatic ovation at the osprey's prowess! They can never have seen an

Kestrels nesting in a pine tree. The young are almost ready to fly.

osprey before. How on earth did they know it was not diving on one of them.

With long tail and sharp pointed wings the kestrel is a true falcon, one of our four British breeding species, along with the peregrine, hobby and merlin. The gyr falcon, although a very occasional visitor to the Highlands during the winter months, is only at best a vagrant, and an extremely rare one at that.

Kestrels, which like all birds of prey suffered severely from the effects of pesticides used in the sixties before many such as DDT were banned, have made a strong comeback, and are most adaptable in the choice of nesting sites, an old crows nest, hollow tree, rock ledge, even cathedrals or other tall buildings – all fill the bill. Recently friends told me of a kestrel nesting in a hole in a tall pine tree on the lawn a short distance from their house. A large branch had broken away during the '87 hurricane leaving a perfect hollow, where the kestrel laid five eggs and reared the whole brood successfully. It was quite an eye-opener to see what food was brought to the young, and whilst field mice, voles and shrews formed the bulk of prey as one would expect, young birds often featured and at one point a baby rabbit. In certain localities lizards, beetles, grasshoppers and other insects will also form part of their summer diet, and yes, they occasionally take very young pheasant and other gamebird chicks as well.

The young were almost ready to fly when I saw them, but seemed completely at ease whilst we were around, though the parent birds kept their distance.

I was reminded of another occasion when I was fishing in Perthshire one September afternoon, when a young kestrel flew up from the grass close to where I had passed with my labrador and settled in a nearby ash tree. I continued to fish down the pool towards the tree when the kestrel flew straight towards me – I thought for a moment it was going to land on my head. Instead it settled on a post in the bank a few yards from us, and sat there quite unconcerned whilst it looked first at me, then my labrador and then to the grassy bank it had vacated. I stopped fishing for a minute or two whilst it just sat where it was, then started casting again, but it was in no hurry to depart, and only took wing when I was almost up to it. It had obviously decided we were both quite harmless, and had not been taught, or yet learnt, to give humans a wide berth. Being such beneficial predators the more encouragement we can give them the better and the countryside has only to benefit from their presence.

A kestrel hovering in still air. On a windy day it hardly moves its wings.

Close encounters

I THINK IT MUST have been the sharp eyes of a blackbird that discovered a tawny owl sitting on a low branch of an ivy-covered oak which led to its being mobbed by a whole host of small birds. The message they were all conveying was straight from the shoulder and after much chivvying and bad language the tawny owl was put to flight. I suppose birds of prey are accustomed to this sort of behaviour, but two little owls which live down the lane spend a great deal of their daylight hours perched unmolested on the telegraph wires and nearby trees, scanning the road for insects. They are probably not averse to taking a shrew or small vole, though small birds seem to know they are not on the menu, whereas they might quite literally be caught napping by a tawny owl after dark.

LEFT
Our resident little owl on the look out.

OPPOSITE
Peregrine – at high speed.

Kestrels too, are seldom at the receiving end of such behaviour, though twice recently I have seen our local resident being mobbed by a crow, which may well have been attempting to get a free meal of a mouse the kestrel had caught, much as a skua will attack a gull to make it disgorge its food.

One of the bravest actions I have seen took place years ago when fishing with a friend in Iceland. A family of merlin falcons were circling above us when a redwing, which we guessed must have had a nest of young in the nearby rock face, flew straight at the nearest merlin, made it swerve and returned to its ledge before any of the others had realised what was happening. It could so easily have ended up as their dinner.

Recently fishing one of the Scottish Highlands most famous lochs with Jack, a long time friend, we were returning home by boat with Evinrude outboard propelling us at a good pace. Jack, looking up towards the near skyline, where the ground rises almost vertically for a thousand feet, spotted a golden eagle gliding serenely along parallel to the ridge above us. Its serenity, however, was short lived for at that precise moment, a peregrine falcon dived almost vertically at it like a bolt from the blue, just as a Spitfire might dive on a bomber, almost skiffing its back as it shot upwards to repeat the performance over and over again. Sometimes the eagle took last-second evasive action with hurried wing flaps before resuming its course. Once or twice the peregrine would vary its tactics, making a much shallower approach at incredible speed from the rear before sailing upwards to revert to almost vertical dives at even greater speed, in its efforts to drive the eagle away, from what it must have considered, its private domain. For all of five minutes we watched enthraled, for it almost seemed the peregrine's repeated attacks were being made for the sheer joy of flying. Never once, watching through powerful binoculars, did the peregrine make contact, though it often seemed inches away, but discretion was undoubtedly the better part of valour and so it went on until finally lost from view.

We returned with no fish – but immensely stimulated by the whole episode, and I almost felt Jack, who had served in the RAF with considerable distinction during the war, would like to have been up there too!

Ptarmigan – a bird of all seasons

SETON GORDON, writing about ptarmigan many years ago, recalled a chapter in one of Fiona MacLeod's books telling of a discussion with a shepherd about what would happen when the sun's fire burned low and the shivering earth froze even at the tropics. The shepherd said that, of one thing he was sure, the ptarmigan would be the last bird alive.

Living around the 3,000 feet mark, and never under 2,000 feet, (except in Iceland, Greenland and over much of the Arctic where they live almost at sea level) ptarmigan lead a truly spartan existence. Not just one night on the mountaintop for them, but a year-round facing elements that bring all the extremes our Scottish climate can produce. Come rain or snow, summer or winter, they brave it out, whilst their fair-weather companions of the longer daylight hours – golden plover, meadow pipits, wheatear and dotterel – either seek lower ground or migrate to warmer climates at the first hint of autumn. Only the mountain hares remain to keep them company and, at the approach of winter, they too don white to blend with the coming snows, which cover the tops for the ensuing months.

Only if the snows come late do ptarmigan stand out like so many snowballs.

Of the bird itself, the one single factor above all others essential to its survival is its quite perfect camouflage at all times of the year. I know of no bird that conceals itself better for, as the seasons pass, so the ptarmigan changes its plumage to blend with its changing surroundings. A series of moults take it from a beautiful variegated golden-brown in the spring and summer, to a pepper-and-salt and softer slate grey in which white begins to predominate at the approach of autumn. By the end of October, it is almost completely white save for the brownish-black tail and dusky shafts of its wing primaries, and it will roost on snow drifts by choice when the ground is not completely snow covered – even its feet are feathered for insulation against the cold. When March comes, a further moult sheds white for spring dress again. It is at this time of year – and particularly does this apply in the Arctic – that the cock bird retains its white plumage often for a month or more so as to draw attention away from the hen as she sets about nesting and sitting on eggs. Truly a bird for all seasons!

The perfection of this camouflage has to be seen to be believed, for their very life depends daily upon it for protection from the golden eagle, peregrine and hill fox. I recall a story told me by one of our neighbours which illustrates this far better than mere details.

He was out with his head stalker and had moved high up to get in on a good beast they had seen earlier. The stag was restless and, thinking they would allow it time to settle, the men sat down to their sandwich lunch. For a good ten minutes they ate and conversed together whilst,

On the alert – adult ptarmigan in autumn plumage.

unknown to them, a ptarmigan lay stock still only two feet away. When at last they spotted it, one of them very slowly and gently reached out and caught it in his hand! I have heard reports of hen birds sitting so tight that they could be lifted off their eggs.

I have experienced this remarkable 'invisibility' myself on numerous occasions. Once, having climbed to the beginnings of ptarmigan ground at about 2,500 feet, I had stooped down to examine a magnificent specimen of stag moss growing at my feet and, as I did so, a covey of ten birds rose all around me.

But perhaps the most fascinating example of their wonderful protective colouring occurred when we were out stalking a couple of years ago and had reached a fair height by lunchtime without seeing a shootable beast. So, taking our sandwiches, we settled down on a comfortable peat hag out of the wind, overlooking a rock face in front of us some 40 to 50 yards away, which we had very carefully scanned with binoculars without seeing a thing, for we had heard an old cock ptarmigan croaking there. I suppose we had been talking quietly together and munching our sandwiches for a good five minutes when, suddenly, and as if by command, the whole rock face came alive with ptarmigan – we counted 22 of them – which, having decided we were obviously harmless, started feeding and preening themselves, stretching their wings and moving about without a care in the world.

One other incident is worth recording. I had climbed up into ptarmigan ground in August with the express purpose of getting a photograph or two of these beautiful birds just coming into the full autumn plumage if I was lucky enough to find them: it is often rather like looking for a needle in a haystack! I had two labradors with me, which started to show interest as soon as we had gained sufficient height so, calling them in and making them sit – no mean feat – I peered cautiously over the dip in the ground ahead. As luck would have it, I saw what looked remarkably like a thin edge of rock set at an angle from a larger one but recognised it as the neck and head of a ptarmigan. Slowly I inched my way round to get a fuller view – and photographs – closing the distance gradually as I went. I suppose we must have watched each other for a good 20 minutes as I took a succession of photographs, waiting now and then for the clouds to pass for better light, and not once, except to turn her head, did the ptarmigan move so much as a feather.

Eventually, having taken a number of 'shots', I got too close even for her comfort and she took wing, taking with her one of her young which had sat

Ptarmigan in flight. In level flight, not even an eagle can outfly them.

stock still at her feet and which I had not seen till the moment of flight. The photographs came out better than I dared hope, but it was not until my son, Jeremy, pointed it out that I saw they showed the young one as well.

Ptarmigan are fond of crouching on the edge of rocks overlooking a ravine or precipice, and sharp eyesight will sometimes reveal the head and neck of a cock bird silhouetted against the sky.

Only if the snows come late will their winter plumage pinpoint them on the grey landscape of stones and rocks like so many large white snowballs, and then indeed they must beware the eagle eye and bless the mists and cloud which at this time of year cover the tops so frequently.

April – the moult from late winter to spring in full progress.

Endowed with great speed – except for duck they have the longest wings of any gamebird in proportion to their body – they fly, grouse-like, on fast wingbeats, but on take-off, especially from a rock ledge or edge of a ravine, have a deceptive dipping flight and swinging up or down the hillface, hug the contours as they fly and no eagle will catch them in level flight. But if your search for ptarmigan is spoilt by a golden eagle quartering the ground or circling it from on high and you see no ptarmigan you can reflect that your eagle has made the grade with virtually no effort but you will have witnessed a magnificent spectacle that few see and many will envy – and your ptarmigan will almost certainly be there another day.

The hills without them would never be quite the same.

Epilogue

I CONSIDER MYSELF immensely fortunate to have been brought up from a very early age to life in the country, alternating between farmlands of the Surrey/Sussex border and the Scottish Highlands.

My father and mother loved the country and all it involved. A love of nature is I think in-built, but it can grow remarkably with help from others and my early school-days in unspoilt country outside Worcester overlooking the Malvern Hills – aided and abetted by a remarkable headmaster and his family and relations – did the rest.

When I was twelve I remember being caught red-handed by the same headmaster with a fellow conspirator, in a vine house catching hornets in a butterfly net and a huge rocket was administered. In the immortal words of *Dad's Army* – 'You stupid boy!' But whilst I learnt my lesson over the extremely nasty sting a hornet can inflict I became ever more intrigued by all the natural world – moths, butterflies, birds, animals, fish and reptiles.

And as I never had a flair for painting I took the lazy way out of recording events with a camera, and being given a Box Brownie at the age of 10, never looked back. Whenever I could, especially in later years I always tried to carry a camera with me. Incredible progress has been made in photography since then, for when I was a boy colour film was not available. Now – 1997 – the cost of colour printing is less than black and white! Fantastic equipment is available (at a price) but I sometimes feel cameras are getting unnecessarily complicated. The best advice I was ever given was to use a tripod wherever possible; it can turn an amateur effort into a professional one.

Vast changes have occurred since I was a boy – the land I loved to roam where highland cattle grazed and hay and wheat were harvested – without sprays, and which was home to large flocks of lapwings in the winter, is now nothing but concrete; the runway and land of Gatwick Airport.

As elsewhere, all in the name of progress and with the spread of urbanization, roads and factories, and the pressure of modern farming – where hedgerows are uprooted to allow production for more and more crops – wildlife inevitably suffers.

But at long last there seems a greater sense of awareness at the danger and destruction that has taken place – let us all hope it comes in time, for like the miner's canary, the warning is there for all but the blind to see, and we will end by destroying this most god-given country.

Index

A wise tawny owl.

A real toadstool.

Fieldfare